£5.25

George Scanlan has been a friend and interpreter to Eric Cantona since his signing for Manchester United, where he also helps Andrei Kanchelskis. George studied languages at Cambridge University and played 4 times in the Varsity match at Wembley in the fifties.

He was on Everton's books from the age of 14 and went on to have a distinguished career with the famous Pegasus team, as well as turning out for Hedon, Corinthian Casuals and Liverpool Marine, where he was also a successful manager in the sixties.

George is well known as a Russian interpreter and has helped England, Scotland, Wales, Ipswich, Arsenal, West Ham, Aston Villa, Liverpool, Everton, Rangers, Celtic, Hearts, Cork and Waterford among others.

Co

© **Grandreams 1995**

Written by George Scanlan
Designed by Leyla Ali
French photographs supplied by Sipa Press

Published by Grandreams Ltd
Jadwin House, 205–211 Kentish Town Road, London NW5 2JU.

Printed in Italy

All facts believed correct at time of going to press.

ntents

Introd

Eric Cantona is one of the most creative footballers in the modern game ... He is also the most controversial player in European soccer.

He has been in the headlines ever since his arrival in England in February 1992 – not only on the back pages, but on the front pages too!

This book takes you through the life and times of football's most charismatic performer ... ERIC CANTONA.

Eric Cantona in 1986, at the age of twenty

Eric Cantona – the man destined to become the most controversial figure in English football – was born in Paris, France, on 24 May 1966.

The capital of France is the centre of all national activities – art, literature, politics, commerce and sport. Football plays a big part in the life of the city, which is home to five top clubs, including the renowned Paris St Germain and Racing Club Paris.

But although he was born there, Eric would not be associated with any of the Paris-based teams throughout his career.

His family roots were in Provence in the South of France, an area to which he remains fiercely and proudly loyal. He was brought up at Caillols which is near Marseille, France's greatest port and her third city after Paris and Lyon.

In order to understand the personality of Eric Cantona, you perhaps need to understand something of Provence. Bathed by the Mediterranean sun, it is a region of twisting vines, lemon, orange, mimosa and eucalyptus trees. The scents and fragrances are of oleander, roses, begonias, orchids, carnations, anemones and hibiscus. Many of the streets are lined with palm and plane trees. Great cliffs tower over deep ravines. Medieval churches abound and there are many ancient walls, turrets and battlements to remind us of times gone by.

Close to Marseilles is the famous Carmargue, where the lagoons are breeding grounds for flamingos and storks and where cowboys on white horses chase black bulls.

The towns of the region are famous too: Avignon, with its famous bridge Aix-en-Provence, with its breath-taking fountains and Nimes, with its Roman amphitheatre, are all great tourist attractions.

Another Provence town close to Eric's heart is Montpellier – the place went wild with delight when he helped the local club win the French Cup in 1990, beating Racing Club Paris against all the odds and against all expectations.

Eric's paternal grandparents came from Sardinia and his mother's parents were Spanish. His father was a keen amateur footballer, a goalkeeper.

Eric is the second of three brothers. The others are Jean-Marie and Joel and both of them are good footballers too – recently Joel had a year's contract with Stockport County, just a few miles away from Old Trafford.

Both are proud of their brother's success and they were at Wembley to see his FA Cup triumph in 1994.

his great idol is Peter Schmeichel), but his talents as a outfield player were soon apparent. He played for the well-known boys' club, Caillols, which runs teams between the ages of 5–15, and has given a start to many French professionals over the years.

Eric's saddest memory of his schoolboy football days is of an incident that happened when he was ten years-old. His team had already won the Cup – and needed a single point from their last league match to secure the 'double'.

With only a few minutes left to play they were 1–0 down, when Eric carved his way right through to the opponents' goal. He was just about to tap in the equaliser when the ref blew the whistle.

Was the match over at the crucial moment? Had time run out? No! Eric's offence was that his bootlace had come untied, and at that level referees insisted that players were properly dressed. By the time it was tied again, the match was over!

Eric Cantona would have to wait until 1994, and live in another country, before he would achieve the glory of an elusive 'Double'!

Eric's father gave his three sons early lessons in kicking and passing a football. Eric remembers his dad teaching him to think ahead, to know what to do with the ball even before he received it – a talent that all great players possess.

Another valuable truth taught by his father, was that the ball can travel quicker than a player. Before understanding that, young Eric had believed that dribbling the ball was the most important thing in soccer.

Like all young boys Eric spent many hours kicking a ball against a wall, or shooting at an imaginary goal.

At first he wanted to be a goalkeeper just like his father (it must be a family trait, because Eric's son, Raphael, wants to keep goal too and

Eric teaches his son Raphael the rudiments of football, just like his own father once did for him

IN THE BEGINNING

ERIC in

*Eric receives
close attention from Leeds
United's David White*

An overhead kick
a la Cantona!

It's there!

ACTION!

Eric hits the deck —
against Wimbledon

Eric Cantona's first major influence in football came from his father who taught him the fundamentals, played with him, and later watched him from the touchline at Caillols.

One of the teachers at Eric's secondary school was Celestin Oliver who had been a member of the French international squad which reached the World Cup semi-finals in 1958. He quickly recognised the youngster's potential – and instilled within him the drive to reach the very top.

Most of the top clubs in France offer promising young players a coaching programme which is combined with study at a local school – and young Cantona was a prime candidate.

Nice was the first club to offer Eric a chance to join them, but he was not very impressed with them. They did not give him any souvenirs – badges, pennants, jerseys – the sort of things which all young boys like to collect.

He also received an invitation from Auxerre and it was there that he fell under the spell of manager Guy Roux, who presented him with a club kit. If Eric's father and Celestin Oliver had shown him the way, it was Guy Roux who would lead him to the big time.

Eric loved the set-up at Auxerre's Abbe Deschamps Stadium, but his parents wanted him to

Eric on the move to Marseille

MARSEILLE

MAKING T

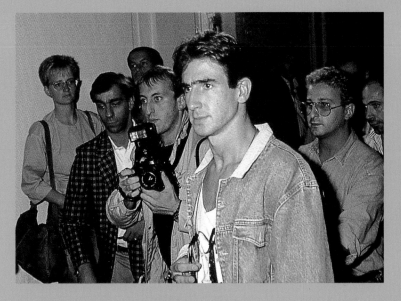

The media began to take note of young M. Cantona

go to Nice which was much closer to home. He was still only fifteen, and they thought he would miss his home and friends. But they also knew that it was in Eric's nature to do what he thought was right – to listen to others, but to think for himself.

As much as he loved his family, he decided to leave home and seek his footballing fortune in Auxerre.

Eric in action for Auxerre against Paris St Germain

HE GRADE

Guy Roux was in the habit of trying out young players against senior players, and he threw Eric Cantona in at the deep end when he was only sixteen. The talented youngster completely outplayed one of the first team players. What's more he wasn't at all phased when the older man tried to exact revenge by using rough tactics.

Watching from the touchline, Guy Roux was satisfied that young Cantona would make the grade in the tough world of professional football.

A magical moment for Eric came with his selection for the French Under-18s team against Switzerland, in Lyon. He thought it was great to be staying in the same hotel as stars like Platini, Giresse and Tigana of senior French team due to play Bulgaria in a friendly on the following evening.

Eric scored in the Under-18s' 3–2 win – and he longed for the day when his own senior debut would come.

Throughout the 1982–83 season he scored 20 goals for Auxerre Reserves who won the Third Division Championship. Then, on 22 October 1983 Guy Roux selected him for his first team debut in a First Division match against Nancy.

He played alongside the Polish international centre forward Szarmach who had helped the club survive its first season in the top division. The wily professional eased the youngster through the game, bringing him into the action with a succession of easy passes. It was a terrific experience and Eric thoroughly enjoyed the 4–1 victory.

At the age of 18, Eric entered the French army for his compulsory year of national service. He was stationed at a special army sports section in Fontainebleu, and was chosen for the French Army side on a tour of West Africa.

He enjoyed army life and was able to let off steam with his close friend Nino Ferrer who also played for Auxerre. Nino got married shortly after

Eric gives the photographers a hand

demob and he invited Eric to the reception. There he met Nino's sister, Isabelle, a Humanities student at the University of Aix-en-Provence.

Guy Roux asked Eric if he would like to go on loan to Martigues, a Second Division side not far from Aix. He readily agreed, knowing that he would be close to Isabelle. They spent a marvellous year together, visiting places of interest and relaxing in each others company.

Roux is a wily old bird, and he knew that the 20-year-old Eric had matured during his national service, and in the stable company of Isabelle. Near the end of the 1985–86 season, while watching him play for Martigues against Lyon, Roux turned to the youngster's father and told him that Eric would be a regular member of the Auxerre first team in 1986–87.

Eric's return to First Division football brought selection for the French Under-21 side – a fantastic team which reached the two-legged Final of the European Under–21 Championship in 1988. In August 1987 he also made his debut for the full French team, scoring in a 2–1 defeat by West Germany in Berlin.

The French press began to take note of him, saying that at last the national team had found the natural attacker that they so desperately needed.

Other French clubs became interested too, and in the summer of 1988, Eric was thrown into the glare of the media spotlight, with a £2 million transfer to the club of his childhood dreams, Olympique Marseille.

Eric later came to admire the expressive Argentinian star, Diego Maradona

Eric's

E ven at the tender age of eight Eric had a footballing idol – the great John Cruyff of Holland. He loved the style and elegance with which the Dutch played the game – and he was unable to sleep on the night in 1974 when West Germany had beaten Holland in the World Cup Final. Four years later he was sad when Holland again lost a World Cup Final, this time against Argentina.

Closer to home Eric was a great fan of his local French League club Olympique Marseille, for whom he would one day play.

In more recent years he has been a great admirer of Diego Maradona. He considers the Argentinian star to be one of the best footballers of all time. Eric was at the 1994 World Cup Finals as a match analyst for French TV – and for him "the lights went out" when Maradona left the stage.

Cruyff later became coach of Spanish giants Barcelona

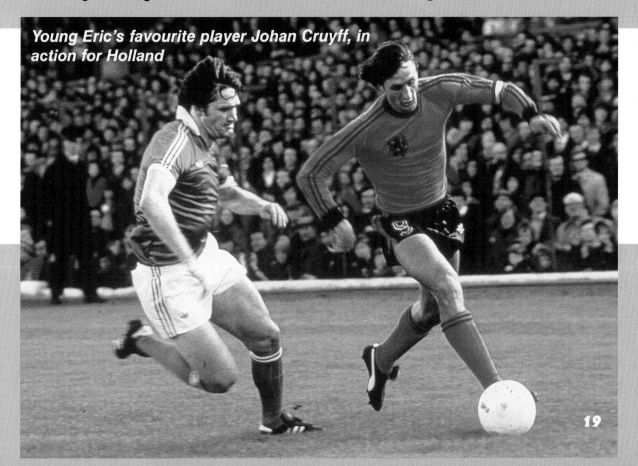

Young Eric's favourite player Johan Cruyff, in action for Holland

19

The French newspapers were looking for a sensation from Olympique Marseille's new star, Eric Cantona. And they got it – when he was left out of the national team by manager Henri Michel. He spoke his mind on the matter and was promptly banned from international football for a year.

More controversy was to follow. In 1989, while playing for Marseille in a friendly against Moscow Torpedo, in aid of the Armenian Disaster Fund, Eric threw his shirt to the ground in disgust at being substituted. He was subsequently suspended by the club's President Bernard Tapie.

Eric was soon on the move once again, first on loan at Bordeaux and then with a transfer to Montpellier. There he had a fight in the dressing room with a team-mate who had allegedly been talking behind his back. Once again Eric was suspended.

On the ball for Marseille again...

ROUBLE ahead!

A spectacular overhead kick while training for France

Eric celebrates a goal for Marseille

But the incident was soon forgotten. Eric was to score the only goal in the 1990 French Cup semi-final against St Etienne.

Montpellier went on to win the Cup, beating Racing Club Paris 2–1 in the Final, at the Parc des Princes in front of 45,000 fans. Bernard Tapie at Marseille realised he had made a great mistake in selling Cantona, and he bought him back for a second time. The shirt-throwing incident was consigned to the past and Eric started the 1990–91 season well, scoring seven goals in the first twelve games.

He returned to the French team and scored in a 2–1 victory over Iceland, in Reykjavik. Then he had bad luck with an injury, sustained when a Breton defender tackled him from behind and damaged his knee ligaments. It was the sort of injury that can ruin a footballer's career.

Eric had been enjoying his football at Marseilles under the management of Franz Beckenbauer. But by the time the player had recovered, Beckenbauer had quit the job after differences with Bernard Tapie. The new manager Raymond Goethals did not pick Eric to play even when he was fit again. The writing was on the wall.

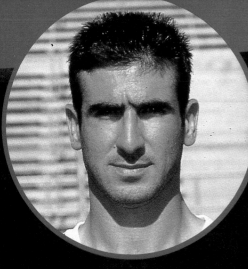

He was transferred to Nimes – a move that was to prove his swansong in France.

In one match with Nimes he threw the ball at the referee and was subsequently called before the disciplinary committee of the French Football Federation who suspended him for a month. To Eric the punishment seemed out of proportion to the offence. He said so, and called the committee members idiots! The ban was increased to two months.

Eric had had enough. He believed he had been singled out for punishment – and he even considered giving up football altogether.

The series of controversial incidents surrounding Eric Cantona had earned him a reputation as 'the bad

The on-loan Cantona at Bordeaux

boy of French football'. But everything had happened spontaneously, on the spur of the moment – there was nothing calculated or sinister about any of his actions.

He would be the first to admit that he should not have done any of those things. It's just part of his character to see things in black and white, to act on impulse and to react strongly if he thinks something is wrong or unjust.

It seemed there were too many people trying to benefit from his impulsive nature. Perhaps he should start again in a different climate? Perhaps he could find pastures new and resume his outstanding career?

Thankfully, there were friends watching his plight, ready to help. They knew football could not afford to lose a genius.

Eric was a great favourite with the Montpellier fans

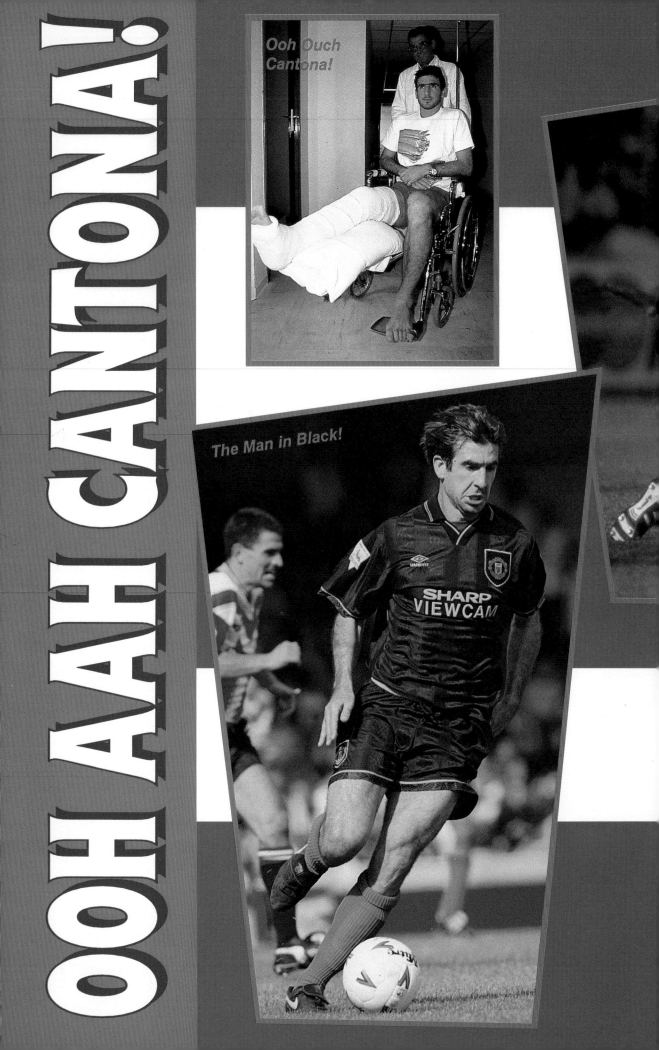

OOH AAH CANTONA!

Ooh Ouch Cantona!

The Man in Black!

The average Turkish defender is the first to pull himself upright.

I wasn't me, ref!

25

Eric celebrates the 1991–92 Championship with his Leeds United team-mates, David Batty and Lee Chapman

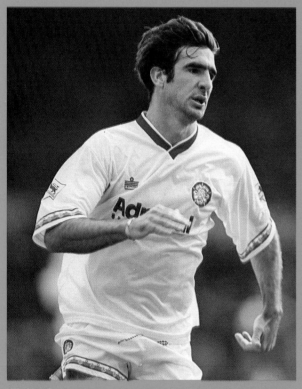

Eric Cantona playing for Leeds United

Bonjour,

ELLAND

Eric's first title success in England, with Leeds in 1992

Cantona receives close attention from Liverpool's David Burrows

ROAD

Eric Cantona's career was saved by one of the world's greatest players, Michel Platini, who had played with him for France and knew his worth.

The manager of the French national side was Gerard Houllier, who had been a student at Liverpool University in the days when the Anfield Reds were winning practically everything on offer.

Both Michel and Gerard felt that England could be the right place for Eric to resume his career. Although no Frenchman had ever made his mark in English football, they believed he was good enough and strong enough to succeed here.

Sheffield Wednesday manager Trevor Francis knew all about Eric Cantona and invited him to Hillsborough for a week with the intention of watching him in action. But Eric thought he was going only for a medical and refused to take part in any trial. The proposed move was off.

Meanwhile, Leeds United manager Howard Wilkinson had just lost his main forward, Lee Chapman, through injury. When he heard of Eric's difficulties, he consulted Michel Platini, took his advice and signed Eric in January 1992. It proved a masterstroke of timing by Wilkinson, whose team was mounting a challenge to Manchester United for the 1991–92 League Championship.

Eric made his Football League debut on 8 February 1992, coming on as a substitute in a 2–0 defeat by Oldham Athletic at Boundary Park. He played in the next League game, a 1–1 draw with Everton at Goodison Park. And on 29 February he came on as a sub for the last 20 minutes of the game against Luton Town, at Elland Road. He scored in the 2–0 victory, and at once became a cult figure in the eyes of the Leeds faithful. By then Lee Chapman had returned to the side and he and Cantona became a dangerous pairing.

As rivals Manchester United became tied up in a congested fixture list (partly because of two earlier victories against Leeds in the Cup competitions), Eric's presence in the Leeds team was giving the Yorkshire side added bite and confidence.

Bonjour,
ELLAND

It was neck-and-neck between the two clubs – until 26 April when Leeds beat Sheffield United 3–2 at Bramall Lane, and Manchester United lost to Liverpool at Anfield. Leeds were the Champions of England for the first time since 1974. Eric Cantona collected his first English medal – and he had only been in the country for three months. And two months before that he had almost given up football altogether!

"Ooh Aah Cantona" was chanted by the ecstatic Leeds fans as Eric took the microphone at the club's celebrations. His own words were brief and touching: 'I love you, I don't know why, but I love you.'

Leeds loved him too. It seemed a marriage made in heaven. But, with Eric Cantona, the unexpected always seems to happen – and so it did.

He was playing well in the 1992–93 season. But as the campaign progressed it became obvious to him that, even though he was the leading scorer, he was not assured of a regular place in the side. At the end of November he let it be known that he was unhappy with the situation at Elland Road.

Meanwhile, Manchester United were looking for someone with the goal touch.

Alex Ferguson had always admired Cantona. Now he pounced …

After spending too much time on the bench with Leeds, Eric moved on …

ROAD

ERIC
AND THE FABULOUS
FANS

Eric Cantona enjoys an exceptional relationship with his fans.

Very few past or present Manchester United players have enjoyed the kind of hero-worship that the French superstar receives.

They know a thing or two about football at Old Trafford, they like class and style – and Eric is mindful of the fact that the fans pay good money to watch matches, and he ensures that he is always in prime condition to turn on a good display for them.

French fans adore him too!

ERIC the RED!

If Eric Cantona had been a New Year gift for Leeds United in January '92, he was certainly an early Christmas present for Manchester United when he crossed The Pennines the following December.

Old Trafford's 'Theatre of Dreams' offered the perfect stage for Eric to display his prodigious talents. And destiny was about to play a part in his life.

Manchester United had not won the Championship for 25 years, and of course they had just missed out in 1991–92.

In the first three games of 1992–93 they had failed to pick up a single point. As the season progressed they were in touch with the leading pack, but it was obvious they were not scoring enough goals. In the seventeen League games before Cantona's arrival they had scored just eighteen goals. That was not Championship-winning form.

Many Manchester United fans had doubts about the arrival of the French star. Perhaps they were taken in by gossip and stories that were simply untrue. Perhaps they imagined he would do no more than rock the boat. In fact he was going to rock the most solid of opposing defences.

Eric signed for Manchester United on Friday 27 November 1993, just in time to travel with his new teammates to Highbury to watch a 1–0 victory over Arsenal. The result hoisted United to fifth place in the table, their highest placing of the season so far.

In the next thirteen games Eric helped inspire United to score 29 goals and become Championship favourites. After his arrival the Red Devils lost just one League game – 1–0 away to Oldham – in which Cantona did not play.

In signing Eric Cantona, Alex Ferguson
effectively saved Manchester United's

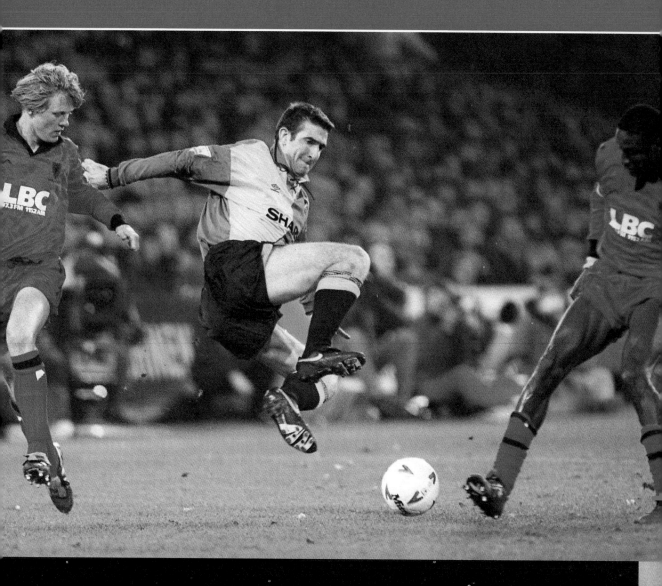

The game against fellow contenders Norwich City, at Carrow Road on 5 April, was a vital one. The season could hinge on the result. In the event the magic of Cantona was too much – he scored the third goal as United destroyed the Canaries with a comprehensive 3–1 win.

That result effectively knocked the stuffing out of any possible rivals. Manchester United won the remaining six games, scoring 13 goals with only three against, and the title returned to Old Trafford for the first time since 1967.

Eric goes flying in his first season with Manchester United

No-one could have written the script. In little over half a season Eric Cantona had become a United star and was hailed as the new King of Old Trafford. Who would have the imagination to even think that Cantona, the outcast, could win Championship medals with two different clubs in successive seasons?

Manchester United's new boy – Eric Cantona

Eric sco

... against Chelsea!

... against Norwich City!

res...

... against Sheffield Wednesday!

... against Arsenal!

37

Eric Cantona had won Championships and Cups in his native France ... In 1991–92 he helped Leeds United win the Football League trophy ... In 1992–93 he inspired Manchester United to become the first-ever Premier League Champions.

Could the Cantona magic continue into 1993–94?

The answer was a resounding 'Yes'. The Manchester United success story continued, and the

Training with the Manchester United squad

club was a hair's breadth away from winning all the domestic trophies.

Eric played 34 games in the Premiership, and he scored a remarkable eighteen goals. United lost only four League games all season, and Cantona did not play in three of them!

In the 2–2 draw with Arsenal on 22 March, Eric was shown the red card following an incident involving Tony Adams. No one except the referee could see anything wrong in the challenge, but off he went.

Although he was allowed to play in the Coca-Cola Cup Final against Aston Villa, the sending-off against the Gunners may have played a part in United's 3–1 defeat at Wembley, as Eric was playing with the knowledge that he would

dou
da

ble
ys

miss the next five games – one of which was an FA Cup semi-final against Oldham Athletic. Eric was a French TV summariser for that game. Imagine his delight when Mark Hughes scored his unforgettable last-gasp equaliser to earn United a replay!

On his return to League action on 23 April, he enhanced his reputation for playing particularly well against Manchester City, by scoring both the goals in the game.

Manchester United eventually finished as Premiership Champions with 92 points, six ahead of Blackburn Rovers. But the last act in a dramatic season belonged to Cantona.

In the FA Cup Final United met Chelsea, the only team to beat them twice that season. United were awarded two penalties and each time Eric strode confidently up to the rain-drenched spot and stroked the ball past the Blues' Russian goalkeeper Dmitri Kharin. Those two goals broke Chelsea's resolve and United went on to a 4–0 victory to become only the sixth club to achieve the glorious 'Double'.

Eric Cantona is the 'King of Old Trafford'. He is treated like a god by United's fans. Yet he is modest about his own contribution to the team's success and is always the first to point out that football is a team game. He is well aware that different players have different gifts – success stems from team play and not from any one individual.

Manchester United has given Eric the kind of 'family' support which he so admires. Old Trafford has been the stage for some of his greatest performances. When the time comes for him to leave, there will be a gap that will be very hard to fill.

After all, there is only one Eric Cantona!

Eric in action for United in the 'Double' winning season

Eric savours the Wembley atmosphere before the 1994 FA Cup Final

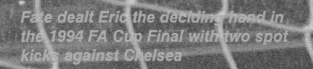
Fate dealt Eric the deciding hand in the 1994 FA Cup Final with two spot kicks against Chelsea

dou
da

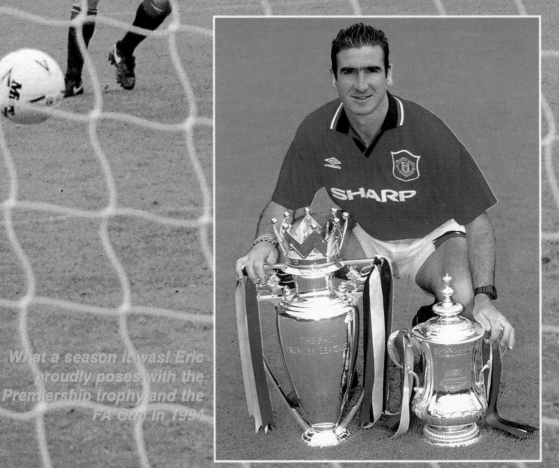
What a season it was! Eric proudly poses with the Premiership trophy and the FA Cup in 1994

ble

ys

another piece of United silverware – the 1994 Charity Shield, after beating Blackburn Rovers 2–0 at Wembley

An Honest Man

Eric Cantona is an honest man who sees everything in straightforward terms…black and white…true or false…right or wrong…good or bad. He admires children for their honesty and absence of deception.

He is a family man. Coming from a kind and loving family himself, he is devoted to his wife Isabelle and son Raphael.

He is also a keen artist who was taught to paint by his father. He donated one of his own paintings to Bryan Robson's Scanner Appeal – and it sold at auction for £1,500.

Those who doubted his loyalty when he first came to Manchester United, did not know him. If people are loyal to him he will not let them down.

Certain journalists, referring to the number of clubs he has played for, were saying that he would soon be on the move again. But they had not looked carefully at the reasons for his previous moves, which were often beyond his control.

Eric is well-liked in the dressing room at Old Trafford. He is not a gossip and would never say a bad word about any of his team-mates. The players know this and respect him for it.

Although he might say that he lives for the moment, that is not to imply that he does not prepare for matches in a way that is a model for all aspiring professionals to follow. He will often stay on for extra training, honing those special skills of his. While he is obviously well aware of his great talent, he also knows that without top level physical preparation, that talent would be wasted.

He enjoys the action in English football and believes that the level here is as good as anywhere else. The future for our national game look rosy to him and he has noted the potential of young players like Nick Barmby, Robbie Fowler and Darren Anderton.

Eric well understands his own temperament. He has a passion inside him which can burst into flame. Often he has been goaded into doing something on the field which gets him into trouble with the referee. His innate honesty has sometimes made him an easy victim of provocation – to a sly remark, an elbow in the ribs, a tap at the ankle – all examples of gamesmanship which often go unnoticed. His reactions are plain to everybody. While he obviously regrets his sometimes rash actions, he does not want to lose that spark of passion in case his whole form is affected.

In January 1994–95 things were going well for Eric. He was sharing the club's top scorer

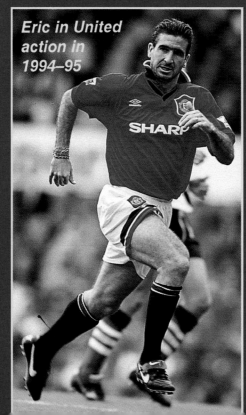

Eric in United action in 1994–95

spot with Andrei Kanchelskis, and United were well placed in the table and looking forward to good runs in both Cup competitions.

The name of Eric Cantona was again selling newspapers. In the FA Cup he had scored a chipped goal of extraordinary brilliance against Sheffield United. In the Premiership the crucial 1–0 win over Blackburn Rovers was the result of a powerful Cantona header.

Then, on 25 January, United travelled to Selhurst Park to take on

Eric and Isabelle

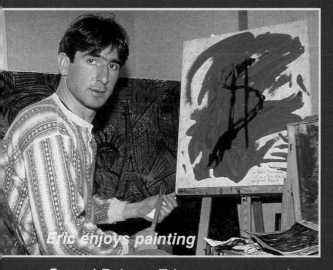
Eric enjoys painting

Crystal Palace. Eric was once again provoked by a series of rough tackles from behind. His temper flared, he kicked out at an opponent and was shown the red card.

As he was leaving the pitch, a Palace fan ran down the steps of the stand, yelling at Cantona.

Cantona reacted angrily – the scenes which followed were televised and photographed for all the world to see.

For several weeks the incident and its aftermath dominated the news. For a while it seemed to many people that Cantona would pack his bags, leave

England and take his abundant skills to Italy.

But every story should have a happy ending - and with his fine sense of timing Eric provided one, at a special press conference at Old Trafford on 28 April 1995. Looking relaxed and at peace with the world, with a twinkle in his eye and the strain of recent weeks gone from his face, he announced that he was staying with Manchester United.

In his hour of need Eric had been moved by the loyalty of his fans. They had chanted his name even when he wasn't playing. They had gone to London to lend their support at his trial and appeal. He was their hero and they begged him to stay.

And, during his community service, the youngsters of Manchester had won Cantona's heart with their expression of affection for him. The honest company of children helped to cleanse his soul of the bitterness of the past - he became rejuvenated by their sense of fun and enthusiasm. They told him to stay.

He did not let them down.

Three young English players greatly admired by Eric Cantona – Nick Barmby, Robbie Fowler and Darren Anderton

Eric
off duty

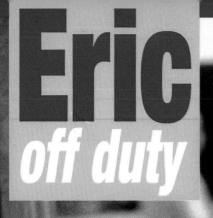

... with his horse!

... on the catwalk!

... with his motorcycle!

Fact ERIC CANTONA FILE

Born: *Paris, 24.5.1966*
Height: *6' 2"*
Weight: *13st 5lbs*

Clubs: *Auxerre, Martigues, Marseille, Bordeaux, Montpellier, Marseille, Nîmes, Leeds United, Manchester United*

French League debut: *22.10.1983 for Auxerre v Nancy, a 4–1 win*

Debut for France: *v West Germany – 12.8.1987, in Berlin. Lost 2–1*

Debut for Leeds United: *v Oldham Athletic – 8.2.1992, at Elland Road. Lost 2–1*

Debut for Manchester United: *v Manchester City - 6.12.92, at home.*

Recent Honours:
1990 French Cup with Montpellier
1991 French League Championship with Marseille
1992 Football League Championship with Leeds United
1993 Premier League Championship with Manchester United
1994 Premier League Championship and FA Cup with Manchester United